WHERE

SPARROWS

WORK

HARD

where sparrows work hard

gary soto

university of pittsburgh press

Published by the University of Pittsburgh Press, Pittsburgh, Pa., 15260
Copyright © 1981, Gary Soto
Feffer and Simons, Inc., London
Manufactured in the United States of America

Library of Congress Cataloging in Publication Data

Soto, Gary.
  Where sparrows work hard.

  (Pitt poetry series)
  I. Title. II. Series.
PS3569.072W5   811'.54   81-50635
ISBN 0-8229-3446-9   AACR2
ISBN 0-8229-5332-3 (pbk.)

Acknowledgment is made to the following periodicals for permission to re-
print some of the poems that appear in this book: *American Poetry Review,
The Missouri Review, North American Review, Revista Chicano-Riqueña,* and
Three Penny Review.

"Bulosan, 1935" originally appeared in *Antaeus.* "Salt," "Chiapas," "The
Widow Perez," "Toward It," "Sueño," "Hitchhiking with a Friend and a Book
That Explains the Pacific Ocean," "Walking with Jackie, Sitting with a Dog,"
and "Her" first appeared in *Poetry,* copyrighted in 1978, 1979, 1980, and 1981
by The Modern Poetry Association, and are reprinted by permission of the
Editor of *Poetry.*

Portions of section three made up the chapbook *Father is a Pillow Tied to a
Broom,* published by Slow Loris Press.

The author wishes to thank the Guggenheim Memorial Foundation and the
University of California for the means by which to complete this collection.
Also, he wishes to thank Chris Buckley, Ernesto Trejo, and Jon Veinberg for
their encouragement, criticism, and friendship.

*The publication of this book is supported by grants
from the National Endowment for the Arts
in Washington, D.C., a Federal agency,
and the Pennsylvania Council on the Arts.*

for Leonard and Omar

CONTENTS

1

2

CONTENTS

1

THE TRUMPET

to Leonard Adame

Again the morning is left to its shadow,
The cat to her paw,
And I'm to a newspaper
Folded on the want ads,
My thumb sliding from job to job:
Milker, roofer, ditchkeeper for the Westside,
Cabbie for downtown, shoeshine at hotel, at carwash . . .
"No way, I ain't going," I puff
At the window, centered with flies. The newspaper
Slapped limp and funneled into a trumpet,
I blow past the coupons,
And the blurred print of obituaries,
But no one hears.

      "Not bad,"
I think. I blow again, my eyes closed
Into knots, and I see myself
In a six-piece band in a mirrored disco in East L. A.
When the bass starts in, the brush
To the snare, the finger to a key,
I'm lost over a few good notes,
And everything is more than just getting by.

THE STREET

Not far
From the cat dropped
By a .22, among
The slouched weeds
Of South Fresno,
Or the old janitor
Pasting bottle caps
Into a scrapbook,
Prieta is a five-year-old
At the kitchen table
Coloring a portrait
Of God, in the blank face
Of a frying pan.

She rings his eyes
Green, beards his chin
In fire, crowns
His head with a halo
That is little more
Than a dinner plate,
Little less
Than the hubcap
Wheeling free
Over the deep ruts
In Malaga.

Where his hands
Reach out, offering
A flower hooded
In the approximate light,
There is scribbling
She tries to undo
With an eraser

And a string of spit.
It never looks right.

†

The shade
Of the back porch,
And Uncle is doing push-ups
On his fists,
His dog tags ticking
Against the cement
Each time he goes down.
When the cat comes
Near, he spits and she steps back
To sniff the air
For the rat who nibbles
Dropped popcorn
In the presence of a broom.
Or it is perhaps the hen
Locked behind wire
Whose filth will scatter
When her neck
Is a loose tube
Of feathers
And her claws
Quiet into roots.

†

Grandmother shuffles
From one fruit tree
To the next, her hands

5

Skinned with dirt,
Her breathing
A hive of gnats.
She is Indian,
My brother believes,
And lassoes her
To a fence
With the rope
That pulled a cow
To its death,
A sow to market,
A piano
To the third floor—
Sparrows circling
As it raised
Past an arena of trees.

Poverty is a pair
Of boots, rain,
Twin holsters slapping
His side, and a hand
Cocked into a pistol.
When he points
And the smoke lifts,
She is gone
In the notch
He scratches into his wrist.

†

I'm the child
In a chinaberry
Flicking matches

6

Into a jar of flies, wingless
And frisking
Themselves empty.
The lid closed,
Smoke knots and unknots
From the hole I poked
So they can breathe.
I shake them,
And they are a raffle
For the ants,
A small cargo
For the wind
To haul into the smeared
Ash of evening.

This will be hours later.
For now, the sun breaks
Above the houses,
Lifting the shadows
On their scaffolds.
A car rattles
From the drive
And stalls in
A great sigh of steam.
I see this and note
That when someone calls
No one has to go.

BURNING MANY THINGS

About that tree on fire,
This puddle, those fields reshuffled by rats,
My thumb passing over a lighter, on a dare.
Something is wrong with me, and it's not my shoes
Or creased shirt, the figure I make
Asking for spare change. Maybe
It's the sun at 6:45
Or my neighbor shaking a chicken
Or the hard breathing of my mailbox
Or the effigy of Santa Claus hanging among my ties.
Yes, something is suspicious, awkward as a crutch,
Blind as the bottle caps pressed to my eyes.
Who can I point to? Dial goodbye?
Now that I've kicked in the TV,
Cornered the cat, and relearned the word *shit*.
How do I look, honey, dancing among the flames?

TOWARD IT

Here are the days
When I could drop a stack of plates,
Overturn chairs, and leave
By the back door

Past my neighbors fanning their iced tea
And the dogs that can't catch
Their breath,
Turning clockwise from where
They're leashed to boredom in the sun.

Something dark under my nails,
And it's not dirt;
Something crawling my spine,
And it's not a fly leading the way

—and there's nothing I can do
About my suspicion of matrimony
That howls behind slammed doors,
But to sweat it out,
Crush a beer can, and watch the choir
Of orange trees bank against the foothills;

Listen to the pigeons shift
And breed like shadows in the eaves,
The sound of shoveling
From the yard,

The graves of our misgivings we build to the end,
As we end unfinished.

MISSION TIRE FACTORY, 1969

All through lunch Peter pinched at his crotch,
And Jesús talked about his tattoos,
And I let the flies crawl my arm, undisturbed,
Thinking it was wrong, a buck sixty-five,
The wash of rubber in our lungs,
The oven we would enter, squinting
—because earlier in the day Manny fell
From his machine, and when we carried him
To the workshed (blood from
Under his shirt, in his pants)
All he could manage, in an ignorance
Outdone only by pain, was to take three dollars
From his wallet, and say:
"Buy some sandwiches. You guys saved my life."

TV IN BLACK AND WHITE

In the mid sixties
We were sentenced to watch
The rich on TV—Donna Reed
High-heeled in the kitchen,
Ozzie Nelson bending
In his eighth season, over golf.
While he swung, we hoed
Fields flagged with cotton
Because we understood a sock
Should have a foot,
A cuff a wrist,
And a cup was always
Smaller than the thirst.
When Donna turned
The steak and onions,
We turned grape trays
In a vineyard
That we worked like an abacus,
A row at a time.

And today the world
Still plots, unravels with
Piano lessons for this child,
Braces for that one—
Gin in the afternoon,
Ice from the bucket . . .
But if the electricity
Fails, in this town,
A store front might
Be smashed, sacks may find
Hands, a whistle
Point the way.

And if someone steps out
With a black and white TV,
It's because we love you Donna,
We miss you Ozzie.

JOEY THE MIDGET

They call him piano-mouth,
Long-sleeve, too-tall-for-the-dogs,
Too-short-for-the-broom.
When someone calls,
He comes smiling,
His hat tilted
Like the axis, eyes red
As the filament in the radio
Dialed to Topeka,
Lubbock, Laramie
On a cold day, Tokyo at noon.

A pencil riding the left ear,
He bicycles downtown
To preach God is the One
And the one
Who steps forward
Will know the feather
That makes an angel fly, the birds sing.
Arms open, he says
"The world is big and you are small.
Look at the Elephant! He has ears
And listens to the ant.
And what about the alligator? His mouth
Is more than yours, but he's not hungry."

At home, before the glow of TV,
It's checkers with a neighbor.
Five moves, ten moves, and the board is closed.
Or it could be shuffleboard,
With bottle caps, against the wall
And the hour that sends

Him to bed, socks
On his hands,
A hot-water-bottle
Saddled to his bad hip
And turning as a dream turns
Through the long night.

†

In the morning
Petals of sunlight pressed to the wall,
Nodding. It's a shoe
For his collie, a bowl of milk
And apricots for the one
Whose mouth is a mail-slot filling
With wind.
       Later,
In the tunneled gray of alleys,
Joey pokes for button jar and toaster,
Rope for the swing,
A pulley for his wash
Foreign with wear.
His march is the ant's march
Far from the hole . . .
And glory to the buckled trash can,
The boxes of pie tins
And car parts, the clear altar
Of bottles brimming with rain.
He bows to what flashes
On the ground, because nothing must go wasted
In a world where sparrows work hard
To prove there is enough.

16

HITCHHIKING WITH A FRIEND
AND A BOOK THAT EXPLAINS
THE PACIFIC OCEAN

On 41, outside Straford,
The sky lengthens magically
When you're 19, the first time
On the road—and if you're
With a friend, the birds lift
And never come down in the same place.
I found myself out there, with Samuel,
Hungry as a fire, kicking rocks,
Under clouds giving up
Just as we came to believe in beauty.
It was that word, and others,
That had us pointing
To windmills and sullen cows,
The trees irresponsible with their shadows.
And it was the eagerness of grass
Under wind, a tumbleweed
Moving, a paper bag moving,
And our minds clear as water
Pooled on roadsides. We went
On for hours. The gravel
Turned under our march,
Until the landscape meant less,
And we grew tired. A banged
Truck stopped for us
And the driver's giddy dog licked
And nuzzled our necks
All through the foothills, toward Pismo Beach.
Two hours, two beers, and the sky
Hazed with mist. When we saw
A rough cut of sea through trees,
We tilted our heads, nudged each
Other's ribs, at the blue
Of waves that would end at our feet.

17

MAKING MONEY: DROUGHT YEAR
IN MINKLER, CALIFORNIA

"It's a '49," Rhinehardt said, and slammed
The screen door, then worked his way around
The dog turds in the yard
To the Buick gutted from fire—the gears
Teething rust, the fenders sloped
Like the shoulders of a fired worker
Out of beer. He circled the car
Kicking the tires, eyeing
The grille that still grinned the ribbed wings
Of a sparrow. He looked inside and flies
Lifted like patted dust, settling
Into a loose knot on the visor.
"Yeh, you're right as right . . . it's a '50,"
Rhinehardt spat, his tongue rolling
A false tooth into place. "It got no
Running board." He pressed a buck
Into his son's hand and retired to the porch
Where he towel-flicked
His wife from a chair
And as evening came on watched beyond
The street, a kennel of trees,
Where—as he had dreamed—a plane would drop
And bloom fire. Two bucks on that one.

THE OUTPATIENTS SELLING BIBLES
IN GOSHEN CITY

They are dropped off, like lumber, in a vacant lot.
In white shirts, shopping bags in hand,
They go in twos door to door,
Shouting "Jesus, God, Praise the Lord!"
They go saying, The end is near—
Sparrows are dying, Indian babies
Are being slammed against trees, in Brazil.
He is coming, they shout,
And the smart ones go outside to look down the street.
Down the street, the White Shirts
Glow on porches, some drooling like hurt snails.
All shouting "Jesus, God, Praise the Lord!"

Downtown, in the clotted throat
Of an alley, dark winos
Who could eat clouds and die from rain
Stare at their shoes, quiet
As the procession passes

Passes barber shop and State Farm Insurance,
Grocery and a furniture store
Bright with flags.
They head to City Hall
Where from behind curtains faces appear,
Frail as thumbprints,
Their eyes squinting at this day given to fire.

At midday the outpatients rest
At a park, in a fence of shade,
Counting Bibles and fingered money,
Staring cats under parked cars,
And housewives behind screen doors and the blare of radios.

An old woman crosses the road with ice water.
A man in a wheelchair motors toward them.
"Everything is love," they shout,
And saucer half-eaten sandwiches to remembering dogs.
The water drunk, prayers said,
What can they do but continue to the next
Street, because there is no bus to pick them up
And sin is everywhere. They
Continue, the woman
And paraplegic joining them,
A man on crutches, a boy with sleeves for arms—
All shaking and crying "Holy, Holy, Lord God Almighty!"

WALKING WITH JACKIE,
SITTING WITH A DOG

Jackie on the porch, shouting for me to come out.
It's Saturday, and I am in a sweater that's
Too large, balled at the elbows, black at the collar.
Laughing, we slam the screen door on a strained
Voice, and run down the street, sticks
In hand, shooing pigeons and the girls
Who are all legs.
                    We cross the gray traffic
Of Belmont, and enter an alley, its quick stream
Of glass blinking in the angled light. We blink,
And throw rocks at things that move,
Slow cat or bough. We grin
Like shovels, and continue on
Because it's Saturday, early as it's ever
Going to get, and we're brothers
To all that's heaved over fences.
Our talk is nonsense: Africa and trees splintered
Into matchsticks, handlebars and the widening targets
Of his sister's breasts, staring us down.
The scattered newspaper, cartwheeling across
A street, is one way to go.
                    And we go into
Another alley, where we find a man, asleep behind
Stacked cardboard. The sun flares
Behind trees and it means little.

We find a dog, hungry and sad as a suitcase kicked open
And showing nothing. At a curb we drape
Him across our laps and quarter an orange—
The juice runs like the tears an onion would give,
If only it opened its eye.
We lick our fingers and realize
That with oranges now and plums four months away,
No one need die.

HEAVEN BOUND ON BICYCLE

for Omar

O.K., then Jesus does have a bad memory
And won't know me from a car salesman
Or a short order cook
Or the applicant who became a shovel.
Listen, it's a short distance to heaven
And self-importance
For I've seen it through a chain-link fence
In the strut of well-dressed blacks,
In a cartwheeling panda,
In the mirrors you've rearranged
To best show your shoes.
I've noted it in the clouds
That slide across rain puddles,
In a calligraphy of kisses,
By the October moon that slipped from its track.
(That night, so much of the sea fell
In the laps of innocent girls.)
And look, I've made the phone book,
You a hotel registry—and don't
We have the faces to be pressed into stamps
And the names to be dropped over dinner
And picked up by dogs on the night wind?
It's clear we're going, amigo, even under assumed names:
I'm Cortes with a road map;
You're Leo da Vinci, beard caught
In the bicycle chain, but pushing on anyway
To the roar of friends shouting Good Luck!

MEXICANS BEGIN JOGGING

At the factory I worked
In the fleck of rubber, under the press
Of an oven yellow with flame,
Until the border patrol opened
Their vans and my boss waved for us to run.
"Over the fence, Soto," he shouted,
And I shouted that I was American.
"No time for lies," he said, and pressed
A dollar in my palm, hurrying me
Through the back door.

Since I was on his time, I ran
And became the wag to a short tail of Mexicans—
Ran past the amazed crowds that lined
The street and blurred like photographs, in rain.
I ran from that industrial road to the soft
Houses where people paled at the turn of an autumn sky.
What could I do but yell *vivas*
To baseball, milkshakes, and those sociologists
Who would clock me
As I jog into the next century
On the power of a great, silly grin.

BROWN LIKE US

for Gerald

"Brown like us,"
Shouts a broom,
The guitar on the couch,
Uncle shooing a wasp
From the house.

Brown like the place
Where I just sat
Watching workers cut grapes into a pan,
Watching a butterfly leaf
Through the vines.

†

Papá, you are a tree
In wind. Your good fruit
Is shook free
And the cats come in two's, smiling.

Papá, your wrist
Is a length of rope, your hands
A wrinkled map of Juárez

Papá, the sun
Is warming my arm and brow,
The garden where I hoed
A grave for the ant.

†

Mamá, the hen
Has eaten her feathers, the sparrow
Her song, our collie a branch
He pulled from the canal.

25

Mamá, the sky
Offers a cloud, the rain
A quick river; this stone
Is like your eye for it's staring at me.

†

Mira, if I cough should I close my eyes?
If a dog licks my hand will he remember me?
Mira, is that hunger or a slow cat?
Is that rain or a glass of weak tea?

†

Who is that man with buckets
For hands,
A razor slash for a smile?
Who is that woman selling brooms
And sweets? Is that her dog
Or is she pointing at me?

†

He is the keeper of the ditches,
Father to a fishbowl, witness to water
Flowing uphill.

She is the stepdaughter
To la llorona, one who knocks on wood,
A sly one calling heads or tails.

†

They tell me it's easy to cartwheel into love,
That under this leaf is another leaf.

They tell me that inside this tree is a canoe,
Down that alley my cat—

Beyond my call, she is no longer mine.

†

"Brown like us,"
Says a shoe,
The penny in my palm,
The accordion wheezing
The end of a corrido.

Brown like the hour
When dogs walk slowly
And mice sidestep our anger
To nibble on rice.

Brown like mi abuela
Who keeps a coffee can
Of seeds and rumor,
A deck of photographs,
Creased and bundled with a rubber band,
In which she is the first one.

CHUY

By telephone,
By rumor,
By the shoe
That grinned ratlike
All the way
To death, Chuy
Called through
A rolled newspaper
Beyond the thin
Scaffolds of trees
Until the trees
Dropped pocked fruit
And the toppled crowns
Of bird nests.
He spoke into a cup
Of dimes, into
A paper bag
That made lunch
Of his voice,
But no answer.
It wasn't until
The eclipse
Of his sad eye
And hunger
For the forgiveness
Of trees
That the stars
Tilted earthward
And his voice
Reached, saying
He was blessed
In the name
Of a violin,

A curled shoe,
The wide stare
Of his buttonhole
That watched
His hands lock
Into a fight
Over the first
Touch of breast.

†

That night his pants
Crossed their legs
And a cockroach felt
What was dropped
From the loose
Tongues of pockets.
It meant the next day
He would sit,
Spoon in hand,
Striking the ants
That unraveled
From spools of dark
Holes. He laughed
When they were
A stain spreading
Into shadows
Trees threw out
Like seed.
He laughed and went
Inside, where
His dog
Was a suitcase of fur

Against the wall,
And the shine
Of a woman's hip
Was a frontier
He crossed before sleep.

†

The next morning
Chuy went on all
Fours, sweeping ants
Into an envelope
He licked and filed
In a coffee can;
He washed
The front window
Where December
Pressed its gray
Face, and blinked
A sadness of rain;
He hooked
A collection of stolen
Hubcaps on the wall
That separated
One dream from another—
Anything to work
Up his appetite
For the apple
That weighed
In his pocket
And kept him from
Floating face-down
Above trees

And the muted houses
Of the poor,
A knot of neighbors
Who pointed from their yards
And grew faint
As a bruise,
While Chuy drifted
And thought, "I knew
It was like this."

†

Chuy fell
For the girl
On a can of peas;
He believed
She was Norwegian
And was back
From the wheat fields,
Her skirt over
A chair, her shoes
On the windowsill
Like lamps.
He saw her reading
By this light
A tale as deep
As the woods
Of the knights
Who failed
To deepen a wound
In Grendel.
They washed
Their hands in dirt

Or spit, strained,
And returned
To a small fire
Where they pinched
Lice from each
Other's beards.
But a poor
Squire, his face
A loose sack,
His wrists
Shackled in sores,
Offered a pocketknife
And asked what
Needed to be cut—
As Chuy popped a pea
Into his mouth.

†

"What about electricity,"
Chuy mused,
Unscrewing a flashlight,
Weighing the batteries
Against the hard
Light of noon.
He thumbed on
A transistor,
A fan that leafed
Through an open Bible,
And the porchlight
Hazed with an orbit
Of gnats. He

Pulled at the ends
Of his moustache,
And sat staring
At the sunlight
That lengthened
Bannerlike
Across the floor.
"Light bends,"
Chuy discovered,
Witnessing the banner
Lift onto the wall
And wave like heat.
Smiling, he washed
His hands flylike,
And wrote in
His journal, *Light*
Is only so strong.
Closing his pen,
Chuy wondered what
He could do after lunch.

†

After lunch
Chuy lay in bed
Thinking about Virginia
And how she danced
That night—
She was a stalk
Of wheat nodding
From the lower lip
Of a farmer;

He was the one
Who leaned on a shoulder
Of cigarette smoke,
Coughing into a paper cup.
When he looked up,
Something fell
From his mouth,
And she turned away.
Later, when
She danced
The *Lava-Bed-Run,*
He blew her a kiss
And crushed a cigarette
In his palm.
Unimpressed, she moved
Into a crowd.
But near the bar,
He said, "The night
Is young, and so are you,"
Slicking back his hair
In the long waves
A sea would envy.
They strolled
To the dance floor
Where he introduced
The *Chuy-Hip-Chug,*
Shoes slipping from under
A rug of beer suds,
Arms waving
Like someone

A mile from shore
And growing breathless.

†

Chuy was downtown
At a cafe, his
Mind on toast or pie.
It was morning
And overdressed
Merchants leaned
Over cup and saucer,
Their words feeding
On the sourness
That brimmed this town.
Chuy noted
On a napkin
—*a street is only so long*—
And stared outside
Where already the day
Had a dog drop
Limp as a dishtowel
And the old staggering
On a crutch
Of fierce heat.
"There is meaning
In that bus, those kids,"
He thought,
And turned the dime
In his coat pocket,

Felt something
Work under his nails.
He noted on the inside
Of a matchbook cover
—*it takes a coin*
To ride a bus—
Paid, and entered
The street
Where he walked
A few brave steps
And propped a crutch
Under his arm.

☨

Armed with an equator
Of fat, shined
Shoes, and a bad
Check, Chuy sat in
The waiting room,
His mouth dry
As a sock,
Thinking he was all right,
That the doctor
Would press here
And there, open
His mouth and offer
Him a toothbrush
And a glass of water.
The doctor would
Tap his knee,
Blow light into

36

His ear, and "umm"
At the milky way
Of moles on his back.
But no! The nurse
Called, told him
To undress, and it was
The doctor's cue
To say, "Looks serious,
My friend, down there."
The doctor glinting
With a needle,
Chuy backed off,
Particularly frightened
Of the cotton ball,
To the window
Where a line of sparrows
Jumped up and down
Like pistons
Which keep the day moving,
Even in a tough time like this.

†

Wherever his flashlight
Poked at night,
In the gutter
Or sloped weeds
Of his yard,
Chuy noted
Things that made
Him stroke his chin
And ask why

He was there,
Under a loose hood
Of stars, believing
That the moon's stillness
Was a lozenge
Sucked before sleep.
He bottled
A leaf, a shaving
Of bark, linked
Worms, and a trumpet
Of snail; he
Snipped a thread
From his lapel
And a lock of hair—
Gifts he buried
In a bottle
Scribbled with his name
So when the sun
Is a monocle
Pocked gray
And earth is lost
To shadow, an explorer
Far from the stars
Would know where he steps
Stepped Chuy, stooping
Among the ruins.

3

CONCHA

This place
Where we lived
Is not far
From your heart.
No! Behind
Your eyes I'm here
Again, a child
In a blue dress,
A chicken under
My arm. My
Brother Jorge
Is at the window
Burning a spider
With a match.
He rubs it between
His palms
And slicks his hair
For good luck.
And I believe
In luck and cross
Myself in the name
Of the goat
Whose little beard
I cut and paste
To my breasts.
I want a hand
To read them
Like braille
Of the story
That begins and ends

At sea, a story
That takes me
Wave over wave,
Salting me
For the long haul
To my next life.

†

Mother is at
The table, counting
The carrots that go
In a soup
1, 2, 3 . . .
She is crazy, I think.
She drools into
A pail, coughs
Into a cup, and drinks.
Her hands are roots
From the garden,
Her smile a slash
In a pig's belly.
I kiss her
And ask about
The chicken.
She nods *Yes*.
I take it out
To the yard, snap
Its neck, and
Under my arm
Press it
Like an accordion

Until the blood
Is flowing
From its beak
And a wine for the dogs.
When I come in
Swinging the chicken
Like a lantern,
Mother is at
The table, counting
1, 2, 3 . . .

✝

Father is a pillow
Tied to a broom
And leaning against
The wall. I
Punch it, saying,
Where are you
Now, you drunk.
I knife him
With a fork
Where his heart
Might be, and
He falls on all
Fours, discovering
Something more
Than blood and a run
Of five fingers.
Of course, this
Never happens.
He is beyond

43

Us, an arcade
For the ant,
A curled negative
In the eyes
Of a lamp.
His hat is now
A pail for the goat,
His coat a flag
We wave at supper.
He is gone,
And I'm here
Behind your closed
Eyes. When they
Open, see how
I'm smiling.

HERMANA

I was waiting
There, in
That doorway,
When he came back
Drunk, a sack
In his hand,
A noosed rope
Over his shoulders.
I stabbed him
Once in the chest
And watched him
Drop into a bundle
Of rags, a heap
Of soiled laundry
A woman might
Prop on her hip.
Nothing else.
No words or screams.
I pushed my
Fingers into his
Wound and he twitched,
Wanting to get up.
I kicked him,
Saying, "Remember
My sister, Greta."
This was last
Week, and already
He is among
The staggered chairs
At the cantina,
While my nephews
Go hungry.

What can I do
But make it deeper?
Their mother is dead
And when he
Comes home, they
Hide behind stove
Or bed, bruised
With the shadow
Of his raised arm.

THE WIDOW PEREZ

After a while
She slumped down in the closet
Among a pile of dirty clothes
To become those creases,
Gray with the meaning
Of wind, black
With the crossing of roads.
For hours she stood
In that musk, between
The slouched shoulders of shirts,
Waiting for you to return,
Your eyes the blurred points
Of twilight, your smile blank
Where a tooth was missing
And lodged with a residue
Of years.
                    But you failed
To come back, old man.
She didn't feel her warmth double
Or tug a sleeve limp
From wear; she didn't touch
Your collar flagged
And gray with distance, your mouth
Sinking into a cup
From which roots lengthen
And push upward
To what the dead say
In a sad flower . . .
Hours later she came out,
Washed, and set the stove blazing.
One bowl or two? The floor ticked
And she turned to listen.

BETO

No, it was Monday
That I ate a sparrow . . .
And Tuesday that I
Slapped a pillowcase
Of frogs against
A fence post, until
They grew silent.
Over where Victor
Was bundled in fever,
Under an awning
Of trees, we made
A fire and pitched
Stones for the big ones—
Over a half-globe
Of flames, their bodies
Bloated like wallets.
We stared into
The sky, in Mendota,
Eclipsed by locust.
When they dropped
We rattled them like seed
In a coffee can
Until they were the mush
That made us sleep.
But that evening
We broke open frogs
Over a towel of smoothed
Leaves. We ate
Their peeled heads
And didn't worry,

Believing the bones, thin
As barbs, might catch
Our sadness
And find a way out.

SUEÑO

"Die while you still have time,"
While summer

Surrenders to fall
And fattened cows to hammer-blows and laughter,

While the days grow mute
And your shadow can afford to take you
To your knees in prayer.

I have nothing to offer
That my slouch will not say better
Or my knuckle admit
To wood,

That my tongue will not frisk
Or my loneliness plead to a totem of stacked coins.

The screen door slams and offers a fly.
The phone rings and it's God
For a small fee,
A man saying it's now or never.
I say "yes," then "no"

And consider a blister brimming in my palm,
Letting the phone drop and corkscrew
Into the next hour
Of television and warm beer.

Later I will rekindle
My interest in the radio's nightshift
Into insomnia

Where, losing count, I'll turn to the window
And look—is it rain or are we all weeping?

SUEÑOS

I am tied to the bumper of a large car.
Four friends. When it picks up speed
We're flying like banners.

†

A baby's face, empty as a glove.
I slip it on,
And I can no longer talk.

†

I'm on a whale's back
Going down, like sleep.
Tiny fish are in my mouth.

†

I'm looking for Mariko
Among reeds, at the turn of a river.
Light is on the water, moving.

†

On the way to a movie,
A condor drops like a coat, nicking my arm.
In the distance, black kids are running bases.

†

I'm at tree level, flying.
If I tighten my belly
I can go higher, even disappear.

†

Out in the Bay
I am drowned, unremembered.
My head, between waves, is a great, dark seed.

51

†

In Mexico a plane goes
Down in buildings.
I'm in another country, growing warm.

†

That man's face is a yard of loose skin.
When he bunches it up,
It's Uncle, back from the dead.

†

My neighbor is now a white person.
Still she won't talk
To me.

†

At the sink
She wants it, tongue here and there.
I give it, and then ask who she is.

†

Chris, Jon, Tim . . .
They've got guns, gray as smeared ash.
No one's talking.

CHIAPAS

There is the one who turns
A spoon over like a letter,
Reading the teeth-marks
Older than his own;

The one who strikes a match,
Its light flowering
In his eyes,
The smoke in his throat;

The one who opens the mouth
Of a dog to listen
To the sea, white-tipped
And blind, feel its way to shore.

At night
They walk in the streets,
The dust skirting their legs
Raw with lice

And the wind funneled
Through a doorway
Where someone might pray
For a loaf of good luck.

†

Somewhere the old follow
Their canes down
A street where the front
Pages of a newspaper

Scuttle faceless
And the three-legged dog hops home.
A door is locked twice
And flies ladder a scale of fish.

Somewhere a window yellows
From a lantern. A child
With fever, swabbed in oils
And mint, his face

Spotted like an egg,
His cry no different
Than the cry
That shakes the trees lean.

A candle is lit for the dead
Two worlds ahead of us all.

LANTERN

Hours late and afraid to go in,
You lay on a couch of raked leaves,
Your thumb stuck in a bottle
Because Father was a blue shadow
In front of TV and Uncle traced
And retraced his tattoos in private.
It was cold in there, hands like a scuttle
Of leaves under exhaust fumes.

You climbed the peach tree and stared over
At the junkyard, at a dog circling
Among the scaffolds of old plumbing.
Far away, a warm length of neon and warehouses
Slamming shut, goggled workers shivering
In broken light. Father called. You turned
And he was below, shirtless, a rolled newspaper . . .
He called again, then went inside
That darkened window by window.

When Uncle shouted promises
You jumped down and didn't know
It was over—the joy of sparrows,
Of rocks you had crayoned faces on,
Of kites falling noiselessly as smoke.
In that quiet you could hear the house
Tick under their footsteps. You raised
The bottle like a lantern at the front window,
And suddenly saw them for the first time
By the same light that gave you away.

THERE

A yard, the pinned wash
White in the wind,
Rattle of bees in a shoe box . . .

I'm looking again
For a brother, his voice over my
Shoulder, behind a shed or the blue caravan of bushes—
Looking for the rain that ends beautifully
In the trees.

Where I played
There are the filth of bottles, gutted mattresses,
A dead cat on its rack of weeds.
My shadow crosses over this heap—
A broken net of flies
Lifts and comes down in knots.

Where my brother squatted over rocks,
The shattered glass and plates
From another year,
A tumbleweed and its raffle of snagged papers.

I sift the glass through my hands
And wheel the tumbleweed into a small fire.
I toss wood chips at pigeons,
Their sounds like a moment faintly remembered.

Toward dusk, toward memory,
The sun banks, silver against the junkyard.
I have much to show—
Bent nails and a pair of pliers.
This coffee-can, pressed to my ear,
Is a way to the sea . . .
Wind in the China tree, and it's just over there.

HER

First I forgot your voice, then the photo you gave me.
When a leaf fell I no longer
Thought of you, shy and wordless, in a raked yard.
I no longer saw you as
The dark girl among trees,
At the entrance to a story for which
The end was always marriage and a bright car.
Your voice never came back; at night
I was left to my nonsense and a typewriter
That couldn't get things right.

This spring, ten years after, we cross
The bay to North Beach
And a bar where we grow sullen with beer.
When I say *remember*
Your eyes reflect, give back
An eagerness that makes me stare into another drink.
Looking up, I take your hand
And it's little more than a warm glove.
I take it, trying to say what it meant, at seventeen,
To lean you in a corner in East Hall
And touch between buttons
As you shivered like a machine, fearful
That someone would see us.

Tonight, no one cares,
And I fail with the light, in reaching.
Drunk, we pay with quarters
And pay again under a wheel of neon.
You hug me like a suitcase
And then send me walking
Slowly back, down a side street,

To a ticketed car and the inevitable "spare change."
On a balcony, a girl
Is singing to the banging of spoons.

ANGEL

Tonight I find the
Calendar with its days
Marked like targets.
It has to do with
The rationed water
Falling from the north
And my woman asleep,
Legs pushed up to
Veined breasts, heavy
And tilting with child.
She turns to expose
The belly rising
—not pure and rubbed white—
But tangled in TV
And telephone poles
Howling through boredom.
My hands patrolling
From throat to hip, I
Think of that good day
When this child will kick
His joints into place
And the eyes circle
An opening room, and close.
Already the fingers bloom
Like candles, the hair
Parts in a warm flow,
And the pocked buttocks
Are globed with fat.
I know this somehow,
Though it is July,

Weeks before our dark
One slides from water
And blood, his blue hands
Tightening on air,
And turns, beyond knowing,
From his life to ours.

BULOSAN, 1935

By train
You rocked past the small towns
Where you might have married
White and worked Mexican,

Or become lost in the Chinatowns
In yellow the tongue,
The brow and the cocked finger—
Yellow and Filipino
Shuffle, the *carabao* walk,
The great arc of urine
Steaming in the cold.

Instead, it was L.A.
A hard cough, and blood on a shirt sleeve,
Pillow and bedsheet
In a room narrow with sunlight.

At the table,
Your eyes two cinders in a fire,
You wrote, but nothing stopped
The black loaf of lung, the axe
Handle crossed hard over your brother.
You wrote:
America is somewhere—
Now touch my hand

Until you dreamed you were a bundle
Of rags slouching
In a doorway,
A bundle poked by a cane and lifted
To a new land.

Bulosan, America slips seaward,
Swallows angle south
Out of reach,

And we step homeward to find
Our lives blue before TV,
Reddened with drink.

Tonight I think of that boxcar
That tunneled south
And you on blackened knuckles and bad knees.

With a finger you were mapping the ox
In the arced horizon, those stars
Drifting west to your country
When nothing could be darker
Than its pull from you.

FRANKIE

Frankie Torres
Corners me
In the lunchroom,
Throws a milk
Carton at my face,
And offers a bite
Of his sandwich,
Fat with the meat
Of sad momma,
Breastless and drunk,
And hanged brother
Cut down
From the rafters
With a grape knife.
It's sour
But I swallow
Fearing the ratchet-
Wind of his fists,
The arc of spit
With girls looking on . . .
We walk out
To the playground;
He wants to be
Friends, shoving me
Against a tree,
Into a pile of leaves.
Lifting me up
We stand so close
His breathing
Is familiar—
Old coat, soiled bedsheet.

He tells me
About sister howling
In a locked closet,
About his dog
Slammed against a tree
By a laughing father.
He leads me
Like a leashed dog
Past the gym
Along the chain-
Link fence, steps
Closer to Spring
When he'll drop
A neighbor
With a 2 by 4,
And I'll drop my sandwich
Meatless and cold.

SALT

for Juan Rodríguez

I

There was nothing to eat, father. We
Were sent out, a sack in our hands,
A stone in each pocket. *Conejo,* mother said,
Frog or catfish. The road was long
But never long enough. We walked toward
The lake that was little more than a mirror
From where we lived. The day
Was clear, and what the wind turned over
We took in our hands and imagined it bread.
We broke this wish in halves, and ate.

II

Some way from home, I threw my stone,
Juan set his sack on fire and it
Was licked with flame. We ran
Toward some cows, fenced but moving.
I wrung their ears, as I might the wash,
But nothing was squeezed into our hands.
They were licking salt rock and rock.
Juan shooed them away. He chipped
A piece off and we sucked until our tongues
Were stropped raw and bleeding.
What was lost, the salt gave back.

PITT POETRY SERIES
Ed Ochester, General Editor

Dannie Abse, *Collected Poems*
Adonis, *The Blood of Adonis*
Jack Anderson, *Toward the Liberation of the Left Hand*
Jon Anderson, *Death & Friends*
Jon Anderson, *In Sepia*
Jon Anderson, *Looking for Jonathan*
John Balaban, *After Our War*
Gerald W. Barrax, *Another Kind of Rain*
Michael Benedikt, *The Badminton at Great Barrington; Or, Gustave Mahler
    & the Chattanooga Choo-Choo*
Michael Burkard, *Ruby for Grief*
Lorna Dee Cervantes, *Emplumada*
Robert Coles, *A Festering Sweetness: Poems of American People*
Leo Connellan, *First Selected Poems*
Fazıl Hüsnü Dağlarca, *Selected Poems*
Norman Dubie, *Alehouse Sonnets*
Norman Dubie, *In the Dead of the Night*
Stuart Dybek, *Brass Knuckles*
Odysseus Elytis, *The Axion Esti*
John Engels, *Blood Mountain*
John Engels, *Signals from the Safety Coffin*
Brendan Galvin, *The Minutes No One Owns*
Brendan Galvin, *No Time for Good Reasons*
Gary Gildner, *Digging for Indians*
Gary Gildner, *First Practice*
Gary Gildner, *Nails*
Gary Gildner, *The Runner*
Mark Halperin, *Backroads*
Patricia Hampl, *Woman Before an Aquarium*
Michael S. Harper, *Song: I Want a Witness*
John Hart, *The Climbers*
Samuel Hazo, *Blood Rights*
Samuel Hazo, *Once for the Last Bandit: New and Previous Poems*
Samuel Hazo, *Quartered*
Gwen Head, *Special Effects*
Gwen Head, *The Ten Thousandth Night*
Milne Holton and Graham W. Reid, eds., *Reading the Ashes: An Anthology of
    the Poetry of Modern Macedonia*
Milne Holton and Paul Vangelisti, eds., *The New Polish Poetry: A Bilingual
    Collection*
David Huddle, *Paper Boy*

Shirley Kaufman, *The Floor Keeps Turning*
Shirley Kaufman, *From One Life to Another*
Shirley Kaufman, *Gold Country*
Ted Kooser, *Sure Signs: New and Selected Poems*
Abba Kovner, *A Canopy in the Desert: Selected Poems*
Paul-Marie Lapointe, *The Terror of the Snows: Selected Poems*
Larry Levis, *Wrecking Crew*
Jim Lindsey, *In Lieu of Mecca*
Tom Lowenstein, tr., *Eskimo Poems from Canada and Greenland*
Archibald MacLeish, *The Great American Fourth of July Parade*
Peter Meinke, *The Night Train and The Golden Bird*
Peter Meinke, *Trying to Surprise God*
Judith Minty, *In the Presence of Mothers*
James Moore, *The New Body*
Carol Muske, *Camouflage*
Leonard Nathan, *Dear Blood*
Kathleen Norris, *The Middle of the World*
Sharon Olds, *Satan Says*
Gregory Pape, *Border Crossings*
Thomas Rabbitt, *Exile*
Ed Roberson, *Etai-Eken*
Ed Roberson, *When Thy King Is A Boy*
Eugene Ruggles, *The Lifeguard in the Snow*
Dennis Scott, *Uncle Time*
Herbert Scott, *Groceries*
Richard Shelton, *The Bus to Veracruz*
Richard Shelton, *Of All the Dirty Words*
Richard Shelton, *You Can't Have Everything*
Gary Soto, *The Elements of San Joaquin*
Gary Soto, *The Tale of Sunlight*
Gary Soto, *Where Sparrows Work Hard*
David Steingass, *American Handbook*
Tomas Tranströmer, *Windows & Stones: Selected Poems*
Alberta T. Turner, *Learning to Count*
Alberta T. Turner, *Lid and Spoon*
Chase Twichell, *Northern Spy*
Constance Urdang, *The Lone Woman and Others*
Cary Waterman, *The Salamander Migration and Other Poems*
Bruce Weigl, *A Romance*
David P. Young, *The Names of a Hare in English*
David P. Young, *Sweating Out the Winter*